"Success is defined differently in every strata of society. Most people in the world define success as being wealthy. They believe it is driving a nice car, owning a beautiful home, family and a thriving career. All of these may represent some level of success. However, success for you, as a believer should be defined by understanding and fulfilling God's divine will and purpose for your life and accomplishing it, excellently!"

As believers our primary focus should be to fulfill our eternal assignment given to us by God; every other achievement should be esteemed as secondary to accomplishing this divine purpose.
#FULFILLINGDIVINEPURPOSE

"But seek ye first the kingdom of God, and his righteousness; and all these things shall be added unto you." (Matthew 6:33)

PROPHETIC INSIGHT #2

"The right spiritual perception helps to create a healthier mindset. If you see the glass half empty you're right... if you see it half full, YOU ARE ALSO RIGHT! Change your outlook on the way you see your circumstances. Begin to see things in alignment with the lens of God. "

Choose how you see the glass; it will determine your overall outcome in life!
#PERCEPTIONDRIVESYOURMINDSET

"Let this mind be in you, which was also in Christ Jesus:"   (Philippians 2:5)

PROPHETIC INSIGHT #3

"You can change your address; you can change your appearance; you can change your job but nothing will truly change in your life until your mindset changes!"

If you take a poor man's mindset into a wealthy neighborhood; eventually you will see old broken down cars in front of the yard. Take time to change, life will thank you for it!
#CHANGEYOURMIND

"Be not conformed to this world but be ye transformed by the renewing of your mind."
(Romans 12:2)

PROPHETIC INSIGHT #4

Thoughts become words;
Words become behavior;
Behavior becomes habits
Habits define your lifestyle!
The words you keep replaying in your mind will eventually control and shape your world!"

Change your thinking and get ready for revolutionary turnaround!
#RESHAPEYOURWORLD

"...whatsoever things are true, whatsoever things are honest, whatsoever things are just, whatsoever things are pure,... think on these things." (Philippians 4:8)

PROPHETIC INSIGHT #5

"In order to bring your dream to life all you need is divine direction from the spirit of God; the right connection and the right measure of faith coupled with patience."

Do not let go of your dreams. Fortify them with prayer and faith then watch them manifest supernaturally by the Spirit of God!
#PUSHFORWARD

"And beside this, giving all diligence, add to your faith virtue; and to virtue knowledge;"
(2 Peter 1:5)

PROPHETIC INSIGHT #6

"When thoughts of failure and discouragement come, you cannot allow yourself to meditate on them. You have been given the power and ability by God to create your own success by having the right mindset."

Negative thinking is like a demonic poison that will corrode your soul. It is important for you to have the skill and ability to accomplish something; however it is more important for you to have the right mindset and believe that you CAN do it...and do it excellently!
#THERIGHTMINDSET

"Trust in the LORD with all thine heart; and lean not unto thine own understanding. In all thy ways acknowledge him, and he shall direct thy paths." (Proverbs 3:5-6)

PROPHETIC INSIGHT #7

"True winners never concede, they are relentless in their fight and will not leave the battlefield until their opponent is defeated and the victory is won!"

You are a true winner. God expects you to operate in the spirit of a kingdom warrior and totally defeat every enemy that seeks to challenge your success in God. The enemies you fail to defeat today will be the enemies that you or your children will have to face tomorrow!
#TRUEWINNERS
#PERSEVERETOTHEEND

"I can do all things through Christ which strengtheneth me." (Philippians 4:13)

PROPHETIC INSIGHT #8

True winners are never defeated; they always find a way to bounce back. Although they are knocked down, they always find the strength to get up and get back in the fight again.

One of the greatest qualities of a true winner is the ability to rebound after you have been knocked down. In the midst of the fight you may be able to land a heavy blow to your enemy but you must be able to bounce back if and when your enemy launches his attack against you. Make tenacity your hallmark!
#BOUNCEBACK

"We are troubled on every side, yet not distressed; we are perplexed, but not in despair; Persecuted, but not forsaken; cast down, but not destroyed." (2 Corinthians 4:8-9)

PROPHETIC INSIGHT #9

"Whenever you get knocked down in life always remember that your enemies may be counting down to your defeat, but God is counting down to the day you rebound. Do not be distracted by the counting, just rise up from the mat with your hands lifted high because you are coming out with the victory!"

Give God praise for your upcoming day of victory. It is much closer than you think!
#GODSGOTYOU

"Put on the whole armor of God that ye may be able to stand against the wiles of the devil."
(Ephesians 6:11)

PROPHETIC INSIGHT #10

"When you were born, you were given an eternal purpose by God to fulfill in the earth. Along with that purpose or assignment, came the proportion and the measure of faith that you would need to bring your God-given assignment to pass."

You have a divine purpose in God that He expects you to achieve. When you were born, not only were you born with a mandate from God, but you were born with everything inside of you to bring it to pass. Once you decide to go after the will of God and pursue it, you will not fail, you will only succeed.
#BORNWITHPURPOSE
#BORNTOWIN

"...according as God has dealt to every man the measure of faith..." (Romans 12:3)

PROPHETIC INSIGHT #11

"Your destiny is the culmination of the God-inspired dreams, visions and ideas you were destined to achieve. Therefore, the truest definition of success is seeking out the divine will of God for your life and fulfilling it."

You will never achieve total success outside of fulfilling the will of God for your life!
#TOTALSUCCESSISINGOD

"Commit to the Lord whatever you do and He shall establish your plans." (Proverbs 16:3)

PROPHETIC INSIGHT #12

"You have the choice either to let your dreams die or make a decision to pray and do whatever it takes to bring them back to life. Whatever you choose, make sure that it will breathe life into everything that you are doing."

The reason God gave you the dream and not someone else is because He knew you could bring it to pass!
#KEEPYOURDREAMSALIVE

"And this is the confidence that we have in him, that, if we ask any thing according to his will, he heareth us:" (1 John 5:14)

PROPHETIC INSIGHT #13

"Every dream or vision has an appointed day or time to be fulfilled. Just as every seed planted in the ground goes through a process of germination before it grows and springs forth; so must your dreams visions and ideas."

If you are able to pass the test of time, you will manifest every promise God gave you...in due season!
#PASSTHETESTOFTIME
#ANAPPOINTEDTIMETOWAIT

"To everything there is a season, and a time to every purpose under the heaven:"
(Ecclesiastes 3:1)

PROPHETIC INSIGHT #14

The spirit of fear is subtle and can attack you when you least expect it. Never allow the spirit of fear to stop you from trying or attempting something great. The only way you can defeat the spirit of fear is by doing exactly what you feel fearful doing.

Fear is one of the greatest enemies of your faith and one of the greatest saboteurs of your destiny. FACE IT! CONFRONT IT! DEFEAT IT!
#JUSTDOIT
#DOITFEARFUL

"For God hath not given us the spirit of fear; but of power, and of love, and of a sound mind."
(2 Timothy 1:7)

PROPHETIC INSIGHT #15

"No matter what your situation looks like, speak the word of God over it; by faith it will change and by His grace you will live."

No matter how it looks, never ever make the mistake of cursing your dreams; what YOU believe, what YOU say will ultimately determine YOUR outcome!
#SPEAKLIFE

"A good man out of the good treasure of his heart bringeth forth that which is good; ..."
(Luke 6:45a)

PROPHETIC INSIGHT #16

"One of the greatest dilemmas you may be faced with as a believer is to not fully understand the power you possess through prayer. You have power, given to you by God, to frame your world, through prayer, and alter your entire destiny."

As a believer, God has given you a powerful tool and spiritual resource through prayer. Effectual, fervent prayer gives you power from God to rearrange your entire destiny!
#POWERTOFRAMEYOURWORLD

"Set a watch, O Lord, before my mouth; keep the door of my lips." (Psalm 141:3)

PROPHETIC INSIGHT #17

"Every farmer knows that for each seed that is planted there is a time when germination and maturity takes place. No matter how long it appears to be taking for your seed to produce a fruit or harvest, it is your job to speak life over it...and wait...it will grow!"

Patience is a well-developed fruit of the spirit. Words of faith are like seeds sown in the realm of the spirit. Be careful to water your seeds with prayer and the Word of God and watch the will and plan of God manifest in your life.
#SPEAKLIFETOYOUROWNSEEDS

"And let us not be weary in well doing: for in due season we shall reap, if we faint not."
(Galatians 6:9)

PROPHETIC INSIGHT #18

If you do not believe in the God of miracles you will never receive anything from Him; when you believe in God then your miracles will begin to manifest without measure.

If you have been trying to accomplish any level of success without God, start believing right now that He is the God who can make every impossible situation possible. Once you maintain your faith in Him, supernatural miracles, signs and wonders will find you!
#GODOFMIRACLES

"You [O Lord] are the God who does wonders; You have demonstrated Your power among the peoples." (Psalm 77:14)

PROPHETIC INSIGHT #19

Your soul comprises of your will, your intellect and your emotions. The pathway to spiritual success is navigated through the lens of a prosperous spirit-filled soul.

You must be vigilant to guard your soul against every negative influence and begin to fill it with the Word of God. Increase the health of your soul by becoming complete in the things of God and you will supernaturally begin to see the manifestation of every promise that He has made to you.
#SUPERNATURALEXPANSION

"Beloved, I wish above all things that thou mayest prosper and be in health, even as thy soul prospereth." (3 John 1:2)

PROPHETIC INSIGHT #20

"Real success does not come because you do not make mistakes in life; rather, the greatest demonstration of real success can be seen in those who have made mistakes and have had the strength to overcome them."

Use your pitfalls as stepping stones to catapult you to the next dimension where you truly desire to be!
#OVERCOMEYOURMISTAKES

"Be strong and of a good courage; for the LORD thy God is with thee whithersoever thou goest." (Joshua 1:9)

PROPHETIC INSIGHT #21

"One of the keys to ultimate success is not necessarily being happy, but rather finding peace, joy and contentment in having a personal relationship with God."

Take time to diligently cultivate an intimate relationship with God and you will unlock the doors to a successful life.
#SUCCESSISINGOD

"But godliness with contentment is great gain."
(1Timothy 6:6)

PROPHETIC INSIGHT #22

"To succeed in life is to exceed and excel beyond the boundaries of every negative expectation, mindset or disposition. It is gaining spiritual power and the ability to accomplish your God-inspired goals."

Go beyond the boundaries confronting you; the sky is no longer the limit!
#EXCEEDANDEXCEL
#TAKETHELIMITSOFF
#NOLIMITSNOBOUNDARIES

"Surely goodness and mercy shall follow me all the days of my life: and I will dwell in the house of the LORD forever." (Psalm 23:6)

PROPHETIC INSIGHT #23

"You must strategically plan your pathway to success. Success or failure is always based on the series of decisions you have made. If you do not plan your success, you have already planned your failure."

Start making the right decisions today; choose wisely and ask the Spirit of God to lead you in the right direction!
#PLANFORSUCCESS
#FAILUREISNOTANOPTION

"If any of you lack wisdom, let him ask of God, that giveth to all [men] liberally, and upbraideth not; and it shall be given him." (James 1:5)

PROPHETIC INSIGHT #24

"Whatever you do in this season, always remember and never forget that even failure is not final. What is final, however, is your decision to finally give up!"

The road to failure is the future blueprint of what not to do as you pursue your path to success!
#FAILUREISNOTFINAL
#LEARNTHELESSON

"Moreover thou shalt say unto them, Thus saith the LORD; Shall they fall, and not arise? Shall he turn away, and not return? (Jeremiah 8:4)

PROPHETIC INSIGHT #25

"If you are going to succeed in life you must have a goal. Each goal must have four basic components in order to achieve it, there must be:

- A Motive – the reason why you want to achieve
- A Purpose - the original intent for which something was created
- An Aim – Your focus/goal/target or pursuit
- And an Objective – how you intend to accomplish your dream

Spend quality time discovering and developing these key components and you would have achieved the hallmark of your success.
#GOALSETTINGCREATESSUCCESS

"A man's heart deviseth his way: but the LORD directeth his steps." (Proverbs 16:9)

PROPHETIC INSIGHT #26

"Once you have established a set goal in life and have sought God concerning it, you must continue to seek God to its completion in order to achieve it."

Most people make the dreadful mistake of stopping in the middle of their journey and never finishing. One of your greatest goals in life should be to finish...AND TO FINISH STRONG!
#GODISYOURANSWERTOSUCCESS
#FINISHSTRONG

"If ye abide in me, and my words abide in you, ye shall ask what ye will, and it shall be done unto you." (John 15:7)

PROPHETIC INSIGHT #27

"Trials, though unforeseen and unexpected, are inevitable. However, they may come to prove you or to promote you. Your ability to overcome your trials is a measure of your durability, reliability and dependability."

Overcoming your trials will undoubtedly elevate you to a higher realm of spiritual attainment in God. Endure and trust God to bring you through them victoriously!
#TRIALSAREPERFORMANCETESTS
#PRESSURETESTEDANDAPPROVED

"If thou faint in the day of adversity, thy strength is small." (Proverbs 24:10)

PROPHETIC INSIGHT #28

"You cannot ascribe to greatness without having to defeat a lion, a tiger or a bear along the way. True warriors don't die! They Fly! They Multiply!"

As you stand in the winner's circle with other great men and women of God, you will discover that your testimony of victory will be similar to those who are standing next to you!
#THEREISAPRICETOPAYFORGREATNESS

"For the LORD your God is he that goeth with you, to fight for you against your enemies, to save you." (Deuteronomy 20:4)

PROPHETIC INSIGHT #29

"As you walk closer and closer to your God-inspired destiny, people are going to have a problem with you....keep walking anyway, even if you are alone."

At times, God may ask you to do something that sounds unique, unusual and uncommon to the average person. People generally tend to challenge, question and sometimes reject something or someone that they do not understand or cannot explain. Regardless of the opinions of men, you must always seek to do what God has called you to do...even if it is unconventional or peculiar.
#STAYFOCUSED
#THEREISAPRICETOPAYFORGREATNESS

"Fear thou not; for I [am] with thee: be not dismayed; for I [am] thy God: I will strengthen thee; yea, I will help thee...." (Isaiah 41:10)

PROPHETIC INSIGHT #30

"People may not celebrate your ascent to the winner's circle, but they will have to respect you for the victories you have won and the obstacles you have overcome to get there."

Your battle scars qualify you to stand in the winner's circle; without fear or doubt that you truly belong there!
#SUCCESSMAKESYOUUNDENYABLE
#SUCCESSMAKESYOUUNFORGETTABLE

"My brethren, count it all joy when ye fall into divers temptations; Knowing this, that the trying of your faith worketh patience."
(James 1:2-3)

PROPHETIC INSIGHT #31

"Along the pathway of success, as you discover how to overcome challenges and dilemmas, you will learn powerful life lessons. These powerful lessons, although they may not all be pleasant, will help to forge Godly character in you and help you to maintain your integrity as you continue to achieve greater dimensions in God.

Your gifts and talents will take you around the world but it is godly character that will keep you there!
#THEPOWEROFLIFESLESSONS

"...until Christ be formed in you,..."
(Galatians 4:19b)

PROPHETIC INSIGHT #32

"Living a successful life will call for integrity at all times. If you can be honest and truthful in the dark, when the light comes on you will not be afraid!"

Integrity is simply doing what is right even when no one is looking.
#INTEGRITY
#DOTHERIGHTTHING

"...till I die I will not remove mine integrity from me." (Job 27:5b)

PROPHETIC INSIGHT #33

"Many people may never believe in you or your dreams and visions; but the day you allow your dream to die is the day you give up and stop believing in yourself."

On the road to success, there may be times when you will have to be your own cheerleader, coach and support team.
#ALWAYSBELEIVEINYOURSELF
#YOUCANDOIT

"...but David encouraged himself in the LORD his God..." (1 Samuel 30:6)

PROPHETIC INSIGHT #34

"Time is one of the most precious commodities that you will ever possess. Stop wasting time and energy trying to prove yourself to people who have already rejected you! Rather, spend more time focusing your prayers and attention on building your dreams. God will honor and reward you for it."

Many times, people come to your life for one of two reasons; to help push you towards your destiny or to help pull you away from your destiny. Don't be distracted by the naysayers. Surround yourself with those who are committed to helping you succeed.
#DONTWASTETIME

And we know that all things work together for good to them that love God, to them who are the called according to his purpose."
(Romans 8:28)

PROPHETIC INSIGHT #35

"Many people waste the majority of their lives wishing for something to happen, not realizing that God has already given them the power, through prayer and faith in Him, to make things happen. Take time out of your busy schedule each day to pray and seek the face of Almighty God. You will then find the power to overcome all challenges."

Many times people complain about something that either they cannot change or that they have the power to overcome. Whatever the circumstance, useless complaining is a waste of time, energy and voice activation power.
#YOURDESTINYISWAITINGONYOU
#MAKEITHAPPEN

"Behold, I give unto you power...over all the power of the enemy:..." (Luke 10:19a)

PROPHETIC INSIGHT #36

"Never argue with fools...especially if they do not respect or understand you! It is a useless exercise of expending valuable oxygen that will only lead to further confusion or frustration. I have discovered that people who generally do not respect you today, if you continue to stand for what you believe, they will have no choice but to honor you tomorrow.

You will never be able to reason or communicate with someone who is not ready or willing to change their minds or attempt to understand what you are saying...it is pointless to engage a conversation with such as a person. Let your life speak for you.
#NEVERARGUEWITHFOOLS
#YOURSUCCESSINLIFESPEAKSFORYOU

"Answer not a fool according to his folly,..."
(Proverbs 26:4)

PROPHETIC INSIGHT #37

"God is never surprised when you are faced with any tragedy or dilemma. He wants you to trust Him in the midst of your experience and believe that He will provide a way for you to overcome it."

Whenever God allows you to be tested, it is always to fulfill a divine purpose. In these instances, God is refining you like gold tried in the fire. Once you are able to endure the process you will come forth as pure gold.
#COMINGOUTGOLD

"Blessed [is] the man that endureth temptation: for when he is tried, he shall receive the crown of life, which the Lord hath promised to them that love him." (James 1:12)

PROPHETIC INSIGHT #38

"Absolutely trusting God is having all odds stacked against you but still having the courage to hold on to whatever God has told you. It is to be resolute and confident in the face of adversity. It is knowing that, regardless of how difficult things may look, God is working all things for your good."

Believing God when everything is going well is not total faith at all. True faith is believing that God is still working all things for good, even when the rug is pulled from beneath you; the bottom falls out and your back is against the wall.
#ABSOLUTELYTRUSTINGGOD
#GODISWORKINGITOUT

"Let us hold fast the profession of our faith without wavering; (for he is faithful that promised;)" (Hebrews 10:23)

PROPHETIC INSIGHT #39

"Your testimony of triumph and victory through belief and confidence in God will catapult you into the Hall of Faith. In the coveted Hall of Faith your success in God can be read by others and bring hope to someone else who may be facing some of the similar struggles you have had to overcome."

There are times you go through things in life which are not just meant to bring you hardship. Sometimes God allows the test because He knows that you can overcome it. He also knows that your testimony of overcoming will encourage someone else to make it through theirs.
#IFIMADEITTHENYOUCANTOO

"But I have prayed for thee, that thy faith fail not: and when thou art converted, strengthen thy brethren..." (Luke 22:32)

PROPHETIC INSIGHT #40

"One of the greatest lessons you can learn on the road to success is how to be grateful. Your first focus of appreciation is towards God and then those who have helped you along the way. Your attitude of gratitude in each season will determine how well you will be received in your following seasons."

When God blesses us, He expects us to acknowledge that He was the one who blessed us and give Him thanks. Learn to always appreciate everything that God does for you. If you learn this spiritual principle, His heart and hand will always be extended to you.
#BEGRATEFUL

"In every thing give thanks: for this is the will of God in Christ Jesus concerning you..."
(1 Thessalonians 5:18)

PROPHETIC INSIGHT #41

"As you go through the shifts and turns on the pathway to success, do not become distracted or frustrated in the middle of your transitions. During these times, God's Protection System (G.P.S.) is simply recalibrating your coordinates to find you the best route to your destination."

Although you prepare for Success, everything may not always go as planned. At times you may see delays, dispositions and other disappointments as unwanted hindrances to your success. However, sudden shifts or deviations to the established plan may be God's way of steering you clear from danger, hardship or unnecessary difficulties.
#GODSGPS

"The LORD is my shepherd; I shall not want. [2] He he leadeth me beside the still waters.
(Psalm 23:1, 2b)

PROPHETIC INSIGHT #42

"In moments of failure it may seem as though you are going under; rather embrace these moments as learning opportunities to assess where you went wrong, what you could have done better and how you can now move forward!"

Seize every opportunity in life to move forward; spiritual stimulation produces divine elevation!
#FAILUREISNEVERFINAL

"...but one thing I do, forgetting those things which are behind and reaching forward to those things which are ahead,..." (Philippians 3:13b)

PROPHETIC INSIGHT #43

"No matter how successful you become, you should always remember to give glory and honor to God for blessing you. You should also understand that your perpetual giving to God keeps the windows of prosperity open. As God blesses you, learn how to bless Him in return, your life will remain in a perpetual supernatural harvest."

God is the ultimate source of all things. The Word of God reveals that it is He that has given us the power to get wealth. Therefore, after He has blessed you, it is only right that you should show your gratitude and bless Him in return. This is how you activate and keep the favor of God in your life.
#BEGRATEFUL
#ACTIVATINGTHEFAVOROFGOD

"Give, and it shall be given unto you; good measure, pressed down, and shaken together, and running over, shall men give into your bosom." (Luke 6:38)

PROPHETIC INSIGHT #44

Press your way beyond the stumbling blocks of fear, your own flesh, doubt and pride. Doubt is one of the greatest enemies of your faith. If you allow the spirit of doubt to influence you, it can cause you to give up on your destiny and your God-given assignment."

There are times in life when you can become your greatest enemy. Many people who may have found the courage to eventually overcome the opinions of other people now find themselves faced with internal struggles that can challenge their overall success. Prayer and faith in God will help you to overcome external and internal struggles as you seek to fulfill your God-given assignment.
#DEFEATINGTHEENEMIESOFYOURFAITH

But let him ask in faith, nothing wavering. For he that wavereth is like a wave of the sea driven with the wind and tossed." (James 1:6)

PROPHETIC INSIGHT #45

"As you pursue your goals and dreams in life, always remember and never forget that God knows how to give you what you need until you have been fully equipped and prepared to handle what you desire."

Almost every sixteen year old wants to own a car. Likewise, almost every thirteen year old girl wants to meet her prince charming and fall in love. However, is either ready to handle what they desire? Just as every father knows his child; our Heavenly Father knows your needs, wants and desires. He will never put more on you than you can handle, be it a trial or a blessing!
#FATHERKNOWSBEST

"...But God is faithful; He will not suffer you to be tempted beyond that which ye are able to bear...."
(1 Corinthians 10:13)

PROPHETIC INSIGHT #46

"Many people make the big mistake of celebrating before they have achieved a definite victory. Many people know how to negotiate the contract but do not have the ability to close the deal. Never go into a relaxed mode until you have successfully prayed your miracle into fruition and manifestation."

When your promise has not fully manifested and you begin to celebrate prematurely, you may eventually become frustrated and disappointed if you do not pray your victory into fruition. Be sure that the key is in your hand, you have already signed the contract, the estate has been signed over in your name and that you have gained total victory before you relax and begin to celebrate!
#PRAYTOTHEEND

"Better is the end of a thing than the beginning thereof: (Ecclesiastes 7:8a)

PROPHETIC INSIGHT #47

"Wealthy people think differently than poor people. While some poor people spend most of their day thinking about how poor they are. Wealthy people, on the other hand, spend most of their day thinking about how much more wealth they can acquire. Great people think great of themselves no matter how low they find themselves. Whatever you think you are you will eventually become. If you believe that you are successful, one day you will be"

Poverty or a poor mindset will keep you hindered and in a perpetual state of bondage! You must begin to make strides towards accomplishing and achieving success in life. The more you experience success, the more you will desire to be successful.
#BECOMEADDICTEDTOSUCCESS

"... and bringing into captivity every thought to the obedience of Christ;" (2 Corinthians 10:5)

PROPHETIC INSIGHT #48

"If you are going to move forward in life, it is very important that you keep your left and right legs functioning in order to move forward because "faith without works is dead."

Walking by faith is a perpetual movement towards fulfilling the will of God for your life. There are so many realms, levels and dimensions in God that, in your natural flesh, you will never be able to attain them all. Therefore your walk of faith is perpetual as you continually attain spiritual success.
#MOVINGFORWARDINFAITH

"...faith without works is dead?"
(James 2:20)

PROPHETIC INSIGHT #49

One of the greatest tragedies in the Body of Christ is not that you are financially challenged; the greatest tragedy is prayerlessness. Many people do not pray! If you, as a believer understood that you have power, through prayer, to call everything to your life, including favor, you will never see another broke day...AGAIN!

God has given every believer power through prayer. Unfortunately, the Body of Christ has not tapped into their spiritual power through prayer and do not realize that God has given the believer a spiritual weapon that can be exercised anywhere and at any time to accomplish everything that they have been called to do.
#COMBATTINGPRAYERLESSNESS

"The effectual fervent prayer of a righteous man availeth much." (James 5:16)

PROPHETIC INSIGHT #50

"Quitting before exercising every level of your spiritual power means that you have robbed yourself of the opportunity to become a spiritual giant. Your journey to success was meant to prosper you in spirit, soul and body. So charter the road to success wisely and you will receive new dimensions of abundant blessings from God."

During the ups and downs of life, God is always on your side. Sometimes the hardest tests in life are designed to help you develop muscles in the realm of the spirit. Not quitting in the midst of difficulties and hardships will help you to become the spiritual giant that God created you to be!
#YOUARESPIRITUALGIANT

"But none of these things move me, neither count I my life dear unto myself, so that I might finish my course with joy,..." (Acts 20:24)

Inspiration For All Kingdom Warriors

DON'T QUIT...

GET BACK IN THE FIGHT!

THIS BOOK WILL:

- Empower you to face every dilemma as a kingdom warrior
- Teach you strategies on how to boldly defeat your giants
- Provide you with keys on how to survive your dry seasons and embrace new ones
- Encourage you to activate your faith, overcoming fear, doubt and failure.

Available Now

- DR. EDISON NOTTAGE -

FOLLOW US ON

Tel: (242) 698-1383 | (888) 825-7568 | www.believersfaith.org

Join

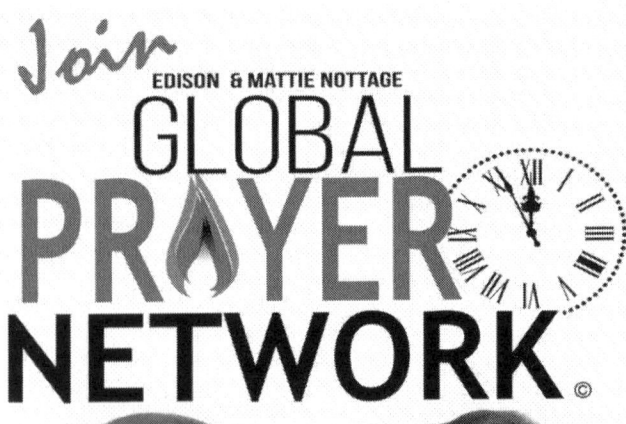

EDISON & MATTIE NOTTAGE
GLOBAL PRAYER NETWORK ©

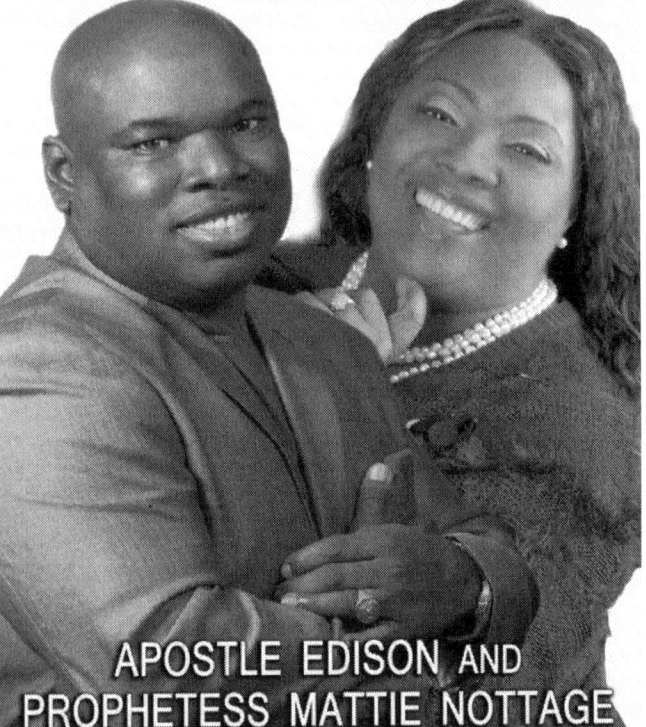

APOSTLE EDISON AND PROPHETESS MATTIE NOTTAGE

www.mattienottage.org

1.888.825.7568 / 242.698.1383

242.812.1070
TEXT/WHATSAPP

To request Dr. Edison Nottage for a speaking engagement, upcoming event, life coaching seminar, mentorship session or to place an order for products, please contact:

Believers Faith Outreach Ministries, Int'l (Bahamas Office)

Carmichael Road, West
P.O. Box SB-52524
Nassau, N. P. Bahamas
Tel/Fax: **(242) 698-1383 or (954) 237-8196**

OR

Edison Nottage Ministries, International (U.S. Address)

6511 Nova Dr., Suite #193
Davie, Florida 33317

Tel/Fax: ***(888) 825-7568***

OR

www.believrsfaith.com

Made in the USA
Columbia, SC
26 November 2017